A BRIEF AND ENDLESS SEA

T0017278

Caitlin Press Inc.
3375 Ponderosa Way
Qualicum Beach, BC V9K 2J8
www.caitlinpress.com

Text design by Sarah Corsie
Cover design by Vici Johnstone
Cover artwork by Phyllis Serota
Edited by Patricia Young
Printed in Canada

Caitlin Press Inc. acknowledges financial support from the Government of Canada and the Canada Council for the Arts, and the Province of British Columbia through the British Columbia Arts Council and the Book Publisher's Tax Credit.

 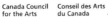 

Library and Archives Canada Cataloguing in Publication

A brief and endless sea / Barbara Pelman.
Pelman, Barbara, author.
Poems.
Canadiana 20230203973 | ISBN 9781773861258 (softcover)
LCC PS8631.E4685 B75 2023 | DDC C811/.6—dc23

A BRIEF AND ENDLESS SEA

poems by

BARBARA PELMAN

CAITLIN PRESS 2023

Now Is the Time to Light It

for Patrick Lane, z'l

Cleansed in the dark where the dead have come for blessing.
The spirit leaves us slowly, forever.
Everywhere the wind covers your passing.

The old lantern by the pond has always been there.
The air breathes like a tree before the dawn.
Cleansed in the dark, the dead have come for blessing,

fly like moths with only night to guide them
and who I am falls behind. The dead gather round you.
Everywhere the wind covers your passing.

Touch their lips with your wings so they may sing,
Be with them what the heart is when it sleeps,
Cleanse the dark and let the dead have blessing.

White moon. The tide. All things receding.
How hard it is to save everything.
Everywhere the wind covers your passing.

Stop losing things I cry, but they keep dropping,
I imagine you in the mountains you call home,
cleansed in the dark where the dead have come for blessing.
Everywhere the wind covers your passing.

all lines taken from poems by Patrick Lane

For Lara and Jed,
always

TABLE OF CONTENTS

*It is necessary and not at all shameful
to take pleasure in the little world*

Ingmar Bergman

I

TYPING CLASS GRADE 10
KING EDWARD HIGH SCHOOL, 1958

Not electric, this one is black,
with round keys: click
and a large carriage return: scree.
Thirty Remingtons create a symphony
of sorts, not in tune, some faster than others.
I sit on a hard wooden chair, straight back,
feet placed just so, hands over the keys
as if I were playing Bach, no not Bach,
some Romantic composer who used the left hand
as melodically as the right:
buy my bunny burn my buggy.
None of my friends are in this classroom with me.
They are in Biology or History or Home Ec,
but here I am, my neat pencil skirt,
tucked shirt with button down collar,
saddle shoes and pink socks:
Young soldier in exile, scree.
We so very leave and hug must.

Girls' Basement Locker Room

Down there, in front of the mirrors, we traded
sweaters and boyfriends, redid

each other's ponytails, prepared ourselves
for the upstairs parade. Showers

connected the lockers to the gym where I learned
the names of football plays—the dive, the sweep—

so I could cheer with precision.
In the cafeteria, a boy I had loved

for four years, ran his finger
along my leg, from white wool socks to the edge

of my pleated skirt, regulation knee length,
not the cheerleading skirts, much shorter.

I perfected the cartwheel and the high kick,
contrived to fail my math exam.

Never impressed by my marks, my mother worried
I was too independent, too smart for my own good.

Meaning marriage, of course. Warning
or prophecy?

But what if I had taken up calculus
and the saxophone, moved to Brooklyn,

what kind of difference would it have made?

A woman sitting alone on a fire escape,
playing jazz to the hot summer night.

First Time

Jericho Beach, 1960

This moment was to change me
from girl to woman. As splendid
as sunrise. As beautiful

as Beethoven. Ode to Joy.
What it was: sand under my thighs,
girdle twisted around one ankle.

You should wash yourself out
when you get home, he said,
you know, a douche.

WILD A LITTLE WHILE

The Hammersmith bus lurched. I was standing,
then falling, against a boy, well, a man,
young like me, not yet twenty-five.
I smiled back at him.
I'm getting off here, he said.
I will too, I said,
because it was summer and London,
and I had nowhere to go.

We went to a park, sat on swings,
sun and sky and the rough fabric
of his shirt against my cheek, the sound
of city birds, and soon the stairs to his flat.
A bedsit, a narrow bed,
a small fridge. A window
overlooking the Thames.

I didn't know his name
didn't know if he was a singer,
an engineer, a day labourer or a clerk—
I was nowhere and everywhere,
a girl with a ticket home
though he begged me to stay.

And the sun rose and fell,
somewhere else. It was day,
it was night. We ate on the bed,
or did we eat anything at all?
I can't remember, just know
we watched stars from the porthole,
that attic ship that sailed
in a brief and endless sea.

CELLO

When he asked if I still loved him, I didn't answer;
but of course, I loved him.
He'd become, by then, like the rhyme scheme between lost
and most.

Carl Phillips, "In a Field, at Sunset"

There was a boy, in Germany, one summer,
he spoke halting English, and I had no German
but we were young enough not to care.
It was August, and along the Spree River,
there was a cello playing. He asked me to dance
and because it was summer, in Germany,
and we were young, I did, and after many days
and nights, we were still humming the tunes from that cello.
I saw him again, just yesterday, so many years later.
When he asked if I still loved him, I didn't answer;

Could I fold the years back? Seal them against time,
which disturbs all the moments we thought we had.
Did we kiss? Of course. Did we talk, then, as now?
There were times when the silence between us
was richer than words, heavier and deeper, as if I knew him
from some other life, but as I said, we were young
and I am less wise now with all my years. Perhaps
the trees leaning into the river, the tall grasses
remember better, those hours after the cello.
But of course, I loved him.

He read me Rilke, I read him Yeats.
Because we had no language, we listened more carefully,
the words rising and falling, like music.
Was it years, or hours ago? The sun on our backs,
the sharp grasses, dragonflies drifting above,
the languid scent of our bodies, deliquescent sun,
such words to stretch along his skin,
his lustrous skin, his eyes solemn, so liquid
he filled me up. As I said, I am less wise now.
He'd become, by then, like the rhyme scheme between lost

and ghost, and I try with words
to pull that summer onto the page,
the long days by the river,
his hands, his spine, the curve of his neck,
the way he woke my skin. And later, at night,
an owl, that low gurgle in the trees above.
And beyond that, the ineffable something
that halts my steps now, along a dark city street
so many years later, a boy I loved the briefest
and most.

NOTRE DAME

Because of a boy with sad green eyes
I miss the gargoyles of Notre Dame,
though I remember his hair, the way it lies
against his collar. The rest, a dream.

I miss the gargoyles of Notre Dame,
but I remember his scarf, the winter breeze
against his collar. Seems like a dream,
my head on his shoulder. I miss the friezes

though I remember the scarf, the way the breeze
lifts his hair. But I miss the arches, the beams.
My head on his shoulder, I can't see the frieze
or the stained-glass windows, the reds, the greens.

His hair through my fingers, I miss the beams,
the beauty of Notre Dame, and later, by degrees
each stained-glass window at Chartres, at Reims
because of his collar, a scarf, a moment's tease.

All the beauty of Notre Dame lost, and later, by degrees
I can't remember his hair. How memory lies!
The touch of his wool scarf, a moment's tease,
because of a boy with sad green eyes.

Peaceful Easy Feeling

lyrics by The Eagles

We took the ferry together, heading to Vancouver,
two young men from California, and they said,
come with us.
It will be fun.

I want to sleep with you in the desert tonight,
with a million stars all around.

The ocean at Carmel, the coastal mountains,
the surf at Cannon Beach, the desert.

I wanted to go with them, wanted
to say yes, let the wind take me where it would go.
I could have loved either of them,
or both—tanned and tender
and handsome—

Got a feeling that I know you
as a lover or a friend

but of course
I said no, said I couldn't
just leave, just like that.

This voice keeps whisperin' in my other ear
Tells me I may never see you again

When I tell this story,
friends shake their heads, say:
Think of what might have happened.

But   yes.
Think of it.

BLUEBERRIES

All right, I will say it then:
I would not have fallen in love again
if it had not been for the blueberries—
acres of them, ripe for picking.
        Laura Apol, "Blueberries"

Three kinds of blueberries in the field,
Erliblue and Draper and Bluecrop,
names I slid along my tongue, tasting.
The sky a cornflower blue.
We gathered handfuls, stuffed our packs
beyond the baskets we brought.
He and I had been friends long ago
and now, fingers blue from picking,
something else, something—
All right, I will say it then:

love. I had guarded against it,
filling my days instead with reading and gardens,
coaxing roses to grow, planting lilac
and lavender, garlic and parsley,
a greening I could pick, pluck, plunder.
It is safer to be alone, I told myself,
avoid the danger the heart longs for.
Foolish heart. I buried it
with the tulips, behind the deer-proof fence.
I would not have fallen in love again

if it had not been a summer day,
if the wind had not been so soft,
if the leaves had not been so full,
if there had been thorns,
if the sun had been too hot,
if it had rained,
if I hadn't brought a hat,
if he hadn't laughed, in just that way,
if he hadn't brushed a stray hair from my eyes.
if it had not been for the blueberries—

We stood in the fields, all around us
green and blue, our clothes stained
and our hair wind-tangled. No one else
along the rows of bush. A call from a jay,
the faint sound of traffic far below.
We fed each other blueberries, one
at a time, our lips blue, our teeth blue,
his fingers in my hair, blue. Blue
slid into our mouths. Blueberries,
acres of them, ripe for picking.

SATURDAY BATH

for Bruce

The large tub, its faucets carefully placed
in the middle, Portuguese tile
and windows looking onto Fulford Harbour.
We sat in the cooling water

and soaped each other's feet,
between each toe, instep, heel,
ankle, the toes again.
It was our most intimate time,

between work and travel and long nights
alone in beds too spacious for one. Those mornings,
no ferry to catch at 6:00 a.m., no plane tickets
in jacket pockets, we'd take our coffee—

poured the way we learned in Lisbon,
milk from one hand, coffee from the other,
the colour just right: not beige or sand
but deeper, caramel. This was before

lattes had leaf drawings or hearts on their surface,
just good strong coffee and milk
in mugs made by local potters,
set onto the counter beside the tub.

Outside the window, a pileated woodpecker,
herring gulls across the water,
occasionally an eagle.
On the beach, starfish, otters.

The tub, the tiles, the coffee, our legs
around each other, smell of sandalwood.
For a few years, a waterfront home,
and all we thought would come with it.

ABJECT

Take me to the place where I can climb no further.
Leave me barefoot in the snow and mapless:
I will come to you.
        Jan Zwicky, introduction to "Forge"

It's appalling, a friend says
when I show the poem to her. That image—

the lover sleeping by the basement door, waiting—
I had thought so beautiful.

Such confidence to lie there, certain she would be taken in,
such courage, if she were not. And what then?

How do these stories end? Total surrender,
Penelope at her weaving, Juliet

with her dagger, Isolde transfigured in death.
Two souls becoming one. Such drivel, my friend says.

Still, I am drawn.

If it were a man, we would call it stalking,
call the police. If it is a woman, we admire her.

And what do you want?
my husband had asked me, one morning

sharing future dreams. He wanted a motorcycle,
a bigger boat, more time. I only wanted to be with him.

After the Divorce

After the empty hangers in the closet,
after the sound of the car down the driveway,
after all the emails, the galaxies of words,

after the visits to lawyers, after the suitcases,
the sorting of possessions—a chair
for him, a couch for you, this painting for him,

that one for you—after the moving vans
and final cleaning, after the real estate agents
and the boxes and the shiny new key,

after the hammering and nailing
and furniture arrangement, after the first sleep
in the new house, after the first planting,

after the dinner parties with odd numbers,
the first visit from daughter, her
needed approval, after the first Passover,

after the hesitant signups:
memoir courses, flute lessons, piano—
after language classes and painting classes,

figure drawing and book making,
writing retreats and editing,
after each book written, the launches—

Who is to say this life,
is not the one you had been waiting for—
your name, bold on the cover.

MAN LEAVES WIFE FOR MUCH YOUNGER WOMAN

I'm writing another story.
No more patient Griselda.
That final night, when he said,
I'm in love with Amy, I would say:
Good, I'm finally free of our vows. Have her.
I've had my suitcase packed
for years. Ticket in my pocket,
heading for blue mountains and deeper seas.
Good luck and thank you. I never
would have left you but I'm very glad to go.

PLEASURE

Eight thousand nerve endings
shaped like two long arms reaching

My mother didn't tell me
I wonder if she even knew

My husband didn't know
nor asked, nor searched

I had no words to tell him
the wonder of it

Both the toucher and the touched
no other function

Not to cleanse or pump or move
or breathe or protect or circulate

Nothing to excrete or mobilize or measure
no other function but pleasure

Ex Culpa

after William Carlos Williams

I've eaten all the strawberries
from the garden we planted.

Forgive me.
I forgot your birthday this year.

Strawberries in a blue bowl
on the pine table
I took from our home

all those delicious years
ago.

II

Lost Names

It isn't our real name, just something shortened by a tired Immigration Officer on Ellis Island, 1914, who heard *Puidelman* and figured *Pelman* was good enough, and easier to spell. Diminished, the family spread across the New World, my grandparents landing on the West Coast where there was a brother, an uncle. *Pelman* on all their documents, *Puidelman* gone for good, along with the *babushkas,* the *samovar* sold for passage money, the embroidered aprons, the long *rhubakha,* linen or silk, the *kokoshnik* decorated with flowers, the *kafkan.* No need for these in this new free land. Perhaps my grandmother kept her collection of *matryoshka* though all that was handed down were her Sabbath candlesticks and a set of Passover dishes. I see her in the kitchen, round bosom, open arms, trying on a name unfamiliar to her childhood, not even the name she accepted marrying the handsome son of the people she worked for—back there, in a town called Minsk, in a place no longer Russia.

PAINTING OF A CHAIR

thanks to Jackie Saunders-Ritchie, her painting

I take my tea carefully,
settle my skirts with one hand,
the teacup and saucer balanced
with the other. There is no room
to stretch out, only to sit
knees together, back straight,
though the chair itself
bends into whorls and curlicues.
We are old, the chair and I,
our bones more iron than bamboo,
more oak than willow.
We have been here a long time,
gathered rust and stories,
lost paint but not dignity.
The tea is a blend of hillside
and heat, a little bergamot,
a little honey. The teacup,
a legacy of grandmothers
who also sat, looking primly out a window
to another country.

Photo of My Mother with My Father

The weeks after he died, my mother
cleaned every drawer and surface of the apartment,
as if she needed to touch
everything he might have touched—
knives, spoons, dishes, sheets,
the towels he would have wrapped around his body,
that body she had held for almost eighty years.

But in this photo, he is still alive.
She is beside him on the arm of his chair,
his head on her shoulder. His eyes are closed.
He is beautiful, his skin
a kind of ethereal, cheekbones
sculpted but not gaunt, white hair smooth.
They are holding hands. My mother
does not smile. Why should she
when her beloved is dying?
Once, when she apologized
for something or other, he shook his head.
You have nothing to apologize for, he said.
you are the only thing I wanted in this life.

SAM'S SHIRT SHOP

On Saturdays my father opened the shop on Hastings Street, between Woodward's where the windows lit up with trains and mechanical elves every Christmas, and Army and Navy where you could get a bargain if you knew what to look for. A tiny store, narrow, shelved to the ceiling with boxes of shirts, ties, socks, sweaters. Sam's Shirt Shop, the name a hand-me-down from the previous owner, but everyone called my dad Sam anyway.

Together we unshrouded the shirts and suits he had carefully covered the night before, straightened the rows of ties, the boxes of socks and cuff links. My job was to pin a ticket on the merchandise, wait on the rare customer if my father was busy. It took all my courage to ask a man if he needed help, though a lack of customers was worse.

Lunchtime was reprieve—I ran down the street to The Oyster Bar, ordered egg sandwiches—sliced egg on shaved lettuce—and milkshakes, chocolate for my dad, vanilla for me. We sat at the back of the store, tried to talk. Shy daughter. Shy father. Crunch of lettuce, slurp of milkshake a substitute for words. After, he laid out bridge hands, taught me solitaire, waited for the ping of the doorbell to break the silence.

BETH ISRAEL SYNAGOGUE, 1955

On High Holidays we gathered outside the wide doors
in our new outfits, crinolines scratching our legs.
Who had the starchiest? Whose shoes
the shiniest? Certainly not mine.
I stood on the edge of the crowd
in my cotton dress, limp crinoline and dull shoes.

The synagogue new then, another sacred space
for the Jewish congregants, soon after the war.
Built in 1948, the pride of the community,
for those who wanted to sit beside wives
who refused to sit in the balcony. They wanted
equality in this country they'd been born into,
not like their parents who'd fled the pogroms
in Russia and Poland, arriving in Vancouver
with their passports and not much else
Now those fathers swayed under prayer shawls.
in the old synagogue down the road,
their immigrant mothers in the balconies, looking on.

Beth Israel with its fortressed walls,
stained-glass windows, the wide staircase
where we lingered, waiting for the service to begin.
Rosh Hashana, and I am twelve.
My dress never velvet or silk or wool,
my shoes never from Ingledew's or Eaton's.
But I was the Choir Leader's daughter
and could sit up in the loft, looking down
on the congregation. Up there,
I could hear my father's voice soaring
above the others, his high tenor
like the Angel Gabriel.

Beth Israel, so different now, renovated
in 1993, its grand staircase gone,
the choir loft gone, my father's voice
an echo in my mind. *Hashkiveinu*
he sang, *let us lie down in peace.*

Chopin Piano Concerto #1, Adagio

You open the door, not sure if dread
or excitement, slowly, slowly.

There is a table set, food
on porcelain dishes.

You reach for a plate, a portion,
and slowly the dishes disappear.

It's always about loss. The song
a lament, an elegy, a requiem.

One bite is all you get. Remember
what it tastes like. Fill your mind

with mango, persimmon, sherbet,
the taste lingers like the last notes

of the adagio. Like the door closing
and the car slowly driving away,

the daughter growing up and moving
across the continent, the father

in his bed, bequeathing you
all his records. The Chopin

piano concertos, the ones
you listened to with him, both of you

wired into earphones. Listen
he said. Listen, as the music fades.

CADDYING FOR MY FATHER

Sunday mornings we would gather the golf clubs, put their little hats on, settle the cart in the back of the big-finned Dodge. Miles and miles, across the Lions Gate Bridge, along Marine Drive with its waterfront homes and seaside cottages, to Gleneagles Country Club—established because Jews weren't allowed at other ones.

My job was to hand my father the correct iron, or wood, pull the cart, keep track of the score. I was ten, more interested in books, preferred to dance. Our conversations were minimal: *Hand me the nine iron please. Did you see where the ball went?* Chances are I was daydreaming, didn't see the ball, but I saw a blackbird in the bushes, imagined it would grant me three wishes. And what would they be? My own bedroom, a new tutu that stuck out like a real ballerina's, a place in the National Ballet school.

WHILE WALKING WITH MY FATHER, LATE FEBRUARY 2006

for my father (1915–2006)

Coyote, Trickster,
why are you present in my world?
Why do you bring winter to my father,
stealing his light, his blue eyes?
What are you doing on a city lawn,
your pelt peeling, your skin bare?
And Father, early spring on your white hair,
What are you doing, dying?

KEYS

My mother has hidden her keys again,
somewhere in the sewing machine,
under her nightgowns, in her jewelry case,
between the books in the bookshelves.
She can't remember where she put them.
Once we found them in the fridge,
under a loaf of bread.
She doesn't trust anyone, she tells us,
blames the helpers who come every day.
My brother chained them to her pocket,
but she ripped them off, broke the zipper.
She is old, so old, and can't remember.
She'll have to stay in her condo then, says my sister,
exasperated, searching the rooms while my mother
follows at her heels, yelling thieves
thieves.

If there was a key to open
what is left of her memory,
if there were words I could find,
to comfort, but what words
I offer are forgotten in an instant,
only the frantic tape repeated and repeated,
thieves thieves, her keys somewhere in her apartment.
under the stacks of newspapers,
or between the faded pictures in the photo albums,
buried among the orchids that somehow survive,
in the freezer or behind the egg container,
or maybe behind the painting of my father
she looks at every day.

Trying to Hold My Tongue

Each day her voice, Darling I'm passing:
on my land line, cell phone, voicemail,

the message always the same, repeated
a dozen times. Not dislodged by logic,

or humour or anger. Whatever I tell her,
she will forget.

Each visit, I grade myself. Usually, it's a fail.
I try different ways to learn patience.

Today I put a photo of my father near me
so that he can admonish me,

Take care of your mother, he told me
but father, how long?

When I walk with her she tells me
that the cars on the street should be in garages,

the city should fix the sidewalks,
the neighbour stole her newspaper,

the helper stole her keys,
or her wedding ring, her earrings,

that I should wear some lipstick,
my grandson get a haircut.

I am ashamed to write this. Other people
are tender to their mothers, grieve their passing.

I fear my mother will outlive me. I will one day
short all the circuits in my body, die in electric rage.

MOTHER, 104

How do you pronounce Covid? my mother asks,
our nightly phone call. She finally remembers
what she read two minutes ago,

When will you come to visit me?

I can't. The virus.
What virus? What?
There is nothing familiar for her

to hang on to.
The world slows
to a speed she knows well—

take a walk, notice the leaves returning,
the crows on the lawn. She used to bring
bread crumbs, but has forgotten that.

When are you coming? When?

LACUNA DAYS

The gap in my mother's mouth, once
just a sexy space between her front teeth,
like the gap-toothed Wife of Bath.
Now age has dropped two front teeth,
chipped off like a cracker folded in half.
She looks in a mirror, asks:
What happened?

Gaps everywhere these days,
missing friends, missing family,
the passenger seat in my car,
downtown streets empty, the bridge—
only a few cars going somewhere.
Gaps in my fridge, butter
low, fresh vegetables, fruit—
Gaps in my memory, what happened
last week? Last month? Was it ever
unlike these lacuna days? I try
to keep a diary but there are gaps
in the days, missing hours where I stared
out the window at bare branches,
waiting for blossom.

Mother, 106

It has taken me this long
to love her again, this small person
with missing teeth and no memory.

I am no longer impatient
when she repeats
what she said a minute ago.

I play Rummy Q with her,
going over the rules again,
helping her each turn.

In between the pages of the newspaper
she reads, the same page every time,
she sleeps.

We take a walk and she looks back,
Where do I live? she asks.
There, I say, on the fourth floor

Slow steps along the pathway,
a rest at the park bench. Look,
she says, such a blue sky.

ABECEDARIAN ANCESTRY

I come from Aunts and uncles who spoke Yiddish
so we kids wouldn't understand,
I come from Bubbies and Zaydes, not Grandmas or Nanas.
I come from beyond the Caucasus Mountains,
out of touch of churches and cathedrals.
I come from doors open for Elijah,
dreidels at Hanukah, dead ancestors:
six million of them.

I come from Egypt, or so the Haggadah tells me
each Passover, crossing the Red Sea,
matzo in my hand, now with butter
and maybe honey. I come from Fantasy and Fairy Tales,
borrowed each week from the Central Library,
Main and Hastings. A child sitting on the worn steps
reading her books.

I come from Grieg's Song of Norway,
the first theatre production I saw, a seven-year-old
who knew then she wanted to dance. And from
Hanukah gelt, and Harrison Hot Springs
where we chased rabbits and smelled sulphur
and imagined our flesh melting from boiling springs.

I am from ink and pens and paper,
from imagination and books read under covers
at night, holding flashlight steady.
I am from Jerusalem, and Jedidiah
is from me, a beautiful gene pool
of blue eyes and lovers of music.

And I am from **K**eefer Street, Vancouver,
my parents finding each other on the streets
behind their immigrant houses,
and I am from **L**ondon, where I lived
for three years, no, only two and a half,
though I like to think I was there longer,
strolling through Hyde Park, crossing
Waterloo Bridge, riding the tube.

And I am from **L**ithuania, where my mother's
mother lost her parents and came to Canada
and I am from **M**insk, where my father's father
married his young servant and took her
to America, to Vancouver. I am not from **N**unavut
or the **N**etherlands or **N**antucket, though
I have visited some, and I am not from **O**ntario
though I went to school there,

but I am from a scattered number of **P**elmans,
whose name is not Pelman but something else
the Ellis Island officials considered unpronounceable,
who live in Vancouver and San Francisco
and New York and Palm Springs,
who like to sing or play violin and golf,

and I am from **P**oetry, a huge land of cliffs
and seashores, oceans and lovers, baskets
of discarded paper and broken pens
and I am from **Q**uestions and No Answers,
querulous sometimes and **q**uick to **q**uarrel.

I am from **R**eaders of books and newspapers
and **R**omantic epics and classics and poetry
of course, and I am from **S**am's Shirt Shop
where I worked for my father in his narrow store,
trying to **s**ell ties to **s**trangers.

and I am from **T**oronto, the University of,
and a family of **t**eachers, still teaching
though there are no students anymore, and
I am from **U**niversities and dark stone hallways
and desks piled with textbooks, and portable
typewriters, and I am from **V**ancouver,
and **V**ictoria, cities by the seashore, ocean
tides my first music,

and I am from **w**hittled down mothers
and **w**ise fathers and the God of **W**orry,
and from **w**ords, all the delicious and **w**onder-
ful and infinite words, and I am from knee **X**-rays
and more X-rays and failed knees and
collapsed knees and I am from **y**earning
and from **y**es, always yes, though I know

I shouldn't, and I am, finally, from **Z**ion,
study **Z**ohar, love puzzles and quizzes
but not jazz.

III

SOONER OR LATER

Only yesterday, it seems, he in Sweden,
I in Victoria, only yesterday
he believed me when I offered him chocolate,
held the spoon to his fibre-optic mouth.
Only yesterday we picked raspberries
in my garden. Only yesterday
I pushed his stroller to Lilla Torg Square, lifted him
into a high chair, fed him rice cereal, bananas.
Only yesterday my daughter's pregnancy,
Only yesterday, my own.
Soon I will be somewhere else, and gone,
but nowhere can I offer such thoughts
to the morning air, breathe it to a darkening sky,
or tell it to my grandson
when we rescue the drowning bee
and watch its six tiny legs wriggle, then stop.
Everything that lives will one day die,
I tell him solemnly, this big lesson for a small boy.
But not you, Bubbie, he assures me. Not you.

TRAVELLING AROUND EUROPE CHASING A TODDLER CHASING BIRDS

Pigeon lover, we crooned, my daughter and I,
bird boy, have another perogy.
That summer we drove through lethargy,
headed from heat in Milan to the cooler parts of Northern Europe.
Every muscle tired from chasing him chasing birds
in the small medieval towns. Odense, Krakow, Riga.

Day after busy day, around the city squares
where musicians played Mozart on glass harps,
jugglers in national dress. In our pockets, a paperback or two
for moments of rest on a park bench, watching the toddler climb
stairs
or chase more birds. We put a bin of toys in each hotel room:
small board books he had already memorized, some Lego,
a rainbow of crayons and paper. Bootlegging a sip of beer
we hid in the pockets of our backpacks
while he napped in the stroller. Desultory conversation,
waiting out an hour's sleep.

We taught him *pigeon, crow, mourning dove, swan.*
His mouth ravenous for language and linguini,
perogy and parakeet.

Eating Tandoori Chicken in Gustav Adolfs Square With Jed

Jackdaw, I tell him. See the black head,
the feathers. Cousin of crow.
Jackdaw, he says,
his two-year-old tongue
savoring the sound, the world
he has entered, the taste of it.

THIS IS NOT ABOUT THE GRANDSON

Don't write about your grandson,
they warn me. It will be Hallmark,
it will be exclamation marks across the page.
The only people who will love
another poem about your grandson
will be other Bubbies, but they
will be determined to outdo you.
Your daughter cringes
and tells you not to use the love emoji,
not to comment at all
when she posts another adorable picture
of the adorable grandson, and adorable
is one of the words not to use.

But look at him, in his muddy buddy,
curly blonde hair under his toque,
blue eyes full of wonder: puddles.
He places one sneakered foot
in this unexpected pond
where there were only sidewalks yesterday.
It splashes. It wets the toes. You can sit in it,
like a cold bathtub. Water everywhere.

Nobody wants to hear about the time
he threw up his beets, was astonished
at the red he created. They have their own stories,
photos on Instagram,
fridges covered with crayon drawings.

Tell me about your travels,
my friends say, eager to hear anything
other than the time my grandson,
watching his toy train circle the Christmas tree,
headlights blazing in the early morning, declared:
I love how the light cleaves the darkness.

CHRISTMAS

The season of lists. The season of debt.
The season of sleepless nights
followed by the season of loans

and worry. These days
I am mostly off everyone's shortbread list.
No longer a husband to buy

expensive gifts for, no longer
a daughter living at home, now
her own home and family. These days

Christmas is a quiet morning,
a walk along a deserted beach,
books I have saved for this time.

It's not my holiday, I remind myself,
childhood Christmases spent away
from everyone else's trees and presents,

content with the eight lights of Hanukah,
small stacks of money and a spinning dreidel.
Nes Gadol Hayah Sham: a great miracle

happened there. Light for eight days,
oil for the Eternal Light. These days
the night creeps closer, my grandson

walks home from school in darkness,
his rainboots dotted
with luminescent stars.

WHAT IT IS

Here's the gist of it, she writes.
My partner wants to stay in Sweden.
I want to come home, to the Coast.
We can't fix this.

And who's to judge? A marriage
sails for a while in calm seas,
then suddenly, sand bars and rocks.
Wreckage everywhere.

I listen, try to be neutral.
Her life, I repeat to myself.
Her strength. What will transpire
is not in my hands.

It's all good, I tell her, echoing my father's words.
You're doing the right thing.
Nothing feckless about her, nothing glib.
Smart daughter, who walks carefully in her world.

Don't be upset, she warns me.
What can a mother do?
That umbilical cord
never severed.

Don't let your heart stiffen, I hope for her.
Keep it open,
its hinges well-oiled with commodious feelings.
Give yourself grace, and time.

Come home to the rain,
to the shoreline, gulls screeching,
driftwood piled on sand.
Wind on your cheeks.

DIFFICULT ADVICE

Isaiah said: God is my greatest comfort,
and my greatest sorrow.
I don't know how to talk about this.

I understand the sorrow part, know about loss,
about injustice. I don't know
where comfort lies.

My friend, now in hospice,
only a few weeks ago making quilts for grandchildren.
Cancer an assassin in her own body.

My daughter, newly a single parent.
So, love doesn't last? she once asked,
my own marriage in shambles at the time.

I write: all mistakes lead to blessings.
As if writing would make it true.
Though I know I am offering a script

that doesn't fit the facts: A mistake is a mistake.
And seldom is there comfort,
not in the soft light above the *Aron Hakodesh*,

not in the rising tide along the seashore
not in the Garry oak meadows,
not even my grandson, his hand in mine,

waiting on the sidewalk
chanting: Left right, no cars.

COMING AND GOING

Each farewell feels like a wrench
that unhinges, untethers.
No solution, except this tension,
this balance. This morning, a storm.
Strong wind as I walk to waterfit class,
carless these days, months, perhaps
years. Stop for a latte, stop to notice
mushrooms on the hillside, the last blue juniper.
The world slows down around me.

My daughter in Vancouver texts:
her son has a cold
and so does she. I should be there,
taking care of them, running errands,
hands on forehead. Instead
I struggle through a poem, one tedious line
at a time, stretching, like the waterfit class,
for an ending. The wind blows.

Just last week, taking photos
of them in Bloedel Conservatory,
walking through the quarry gardens.
Dinner with family, brief conversations,
never enough words to say to my daughter,
who considers me nosy. Wanting to know
about her life. But the door closes
after I ask: how are you doing? Fine, she says.
Always the desire for more.

I pace the corridor
like a treadmill, listen to the rain.

DYING ALONE

Living alone, I might die alone,
some morning before sunrise,

the moon low in an indigo sky.
Sleep covers a stopped heart.

No signs, no cues to alert me,
the phone useless beside my bed.

Just a slow descent, first the heart,
then the breath—then the brain,

a dream of meadows
now opens to a galaxy of stars.

How many days before someone
wonders why I missed my lunch date,

fitness class, why I don't answer
their emails, or text, or comment

on Facebook. No family
goodbyes, no daughter or grandson

sitting by my side, no last words.
Already just a body.

The soul without company
to help it grieve.

TRUTH

after "Lies I Tell" by Sara Borjas

A woman becomes a mother whether or not she is prepared: that is the truth. A woman tries not to follow the patterns of her own mother: that is the truth. Some women read books on the topic, some talk to friends, some go by instinct. All these are true. A child lives by instinct alone: truth. A child follows her mother's instructions or rebels. Both are true at different times. A slap on the cheek in winter leaves a hard red imprint: that is the truth. An event from decades ago lives in the patterns of today: a truth hard to admit. A mother loves her child: truth. Anger does not negate love: truth. The face is a window to the truth; the child reads the truth in the face, in the gesture. Truth. Truth. The past lives in the present, builds each moment from its bricks and mortar. What erases a red imprint on a child's cheek? A cold day, a child running from her mother.

IV

About Memory

from talks with Rabbi Harry Brechner

Memories are subjective

My mother remembers it like this:
I was standing there, after Sunday School,
and he saw me. I was twelve. Bashert: destiny.
But years ago, before her memory died,
the story went like this: how they were friends,
how he brought his girlfriends to her house—
her parents at work, the house empty—
she in the kitchen, he on the couch with the latest girlfriend.
And how, one day, he said he came to see her, just her.
And that was that, she told us.
Almost eighty years together.

I ponder the stories, wonder why,
even knowing the other, she prefers the first.
The simpler love. Just one look.

∞∞∞

We are what we remember

Every day my mother gets thinner.
Not her body, but the weight of memory.
I forget, she says.
She calls my grandson the little guy,
forgetting his name. She forgets
our stories, who my sister is married to,
the names of her great grandchildren,
what she read yesterday or a minute ago.
She can't remember where we once lived,
thinks it is across town, or the next block.
Who is she now? Not the woman I argued with
every day of my childhood, not the woman

who played piano each evening, not even
the woman my father loved, so many years.
Perhaps somewhere in those diminishing brain cells
she is still the young woman with four children
longing for a larger house, a job of her own,
something else she could never name.

∞∞∞∞

Memories change as we work on our selves

As a child, I had no conversation with my father.
I thought he was aloof. Distant. Even
critical. In my teens, there were no discussions
about love. He could have told me
how to build it, how to repair it when, crushed,
it sulks in a corner. I wish I had coaxed words
from him, could have broken through
what I know now as shyness. But today,
wherever he is, he answers me from somewhere
deep in parts of myself I'm getting to know.
I am with you, he says. You are right.
Open those fists: Potayach et yodecha*.
Have courage.

*Hebrew: open your hands

∞∞∞∞

We ritualize memory

Parsha Yitro. My father's parsha* he chanted
for his Bar Mitzvah. He died near his birthday,
like Shakespeare, like the poet Patrick Lane.
A cycle completed. We women who lost a father
in winter, gather our memories and honour them.

At the Fathers' Kiddush,
we chant, we bless, we tell our stories.
How my family went every summer
to a cottage on Bowen Island, fed the ducks,
sat on the wharf and tried to fish. How I lugged
the golf cart while he called for an iron, a wood,
the small white ball lost in the trees.

*a portion of the Bible read each week

∞∞∞∞

Is it a real memory? Is it a true memory?

I tell a story: a night in Amalfi,
a lover— a cellist—
some wine, some music. Dancing.
Making love deep into the night.
Did it happen? Instead, I wrote poems
about Marcello, and in this way
the story is true. I add details
about the olive trees, jasmine in pots,
dinner of tagliatelle, clam sauce,
the tarantella he played and I danced to.
The early morning walk through the tunnels
of Amalfi. Dawn, farewell.
Did it happen? Is it real? It is true.

∞∞∞∞

Memory is our interpretation of experience

While I was married, we marvelled at the wedding,
how perfect it had seemed, our friends gathered
in a small room, flowers from the neighbours' gardens,
wedding cake from his sister. How it all fell into place,

and after, a midnight glide across Shawnigan lake,
oars dipping like a lullaby. How differently
I remember it now, the best man hungover,
my wedding dress a shade of copper, not white,
heading down the stairs clutching my father's arm
to Tchaikovsky's booming Piano Concerto.
Elephant music, not Shubert, not Vivaldi.
Nothing that happened that day had been planned by me.
I was too busy. In the days and weeks before,
I went to work, cooked dinner, took care of my child.
Last minute choices: music, flowers,
perhaps even him.

∞∞∞∞

Trauma lives in the body

Is it in your throat,
        umbilical cord stretched around your neck?
Is it in your stomach,
        that unexpected punch that knocked you cold?
Is it on your torso,
        boiling spilling chicken broth?
Is it in your fingers,
        the touch from a dead friend?
Is it in your legs,
        that fall, that tumble over cliff?
Is it in your eyes,
        the heat of that fire, the forest, burning?
Is it in your knees,
        how you were held, bent over, crushed?
Is it in your heart,
        like glass, breaking?

V

STAR MAGNOLIA, FIRST BUDS AT MY WINDOW

Each spring is a surprise.
In the garden, magnolia is the first.

This is nothing new, but every year
for a little while, it pushes back news:

grenades fired at children,
babies born in hospital basements,

makeshift schools set up in subways—
mass graves.

Forgive me, distant wars, says Szymborska,
for bringing flowers home. Long fingers of white

against the dark.

Aubade Four A.M.

The moon is low behind the trees,
almost full, hanging like a Christmas decoration
from a higher branch. Too early to wake,
too late for sleep, the time for what-ifs
and should'ves. I have learned not to offer them
room and board. Still, they tap at the window.
The moon slides further behind the trees,
the light slowly lifts:
grass, rock, first birds.

IF BIRDS WERE BIG

after the painting by Emil Nolde Child and Large Bird

If they were the size of horses
roaming the back lawn, or nesting
in the hardiest trees. If their droppings
could kill, like a stone from a tenth floor
window. If they could split you
like an earthworm, scoop you
into a pelican's beak, mash you
into pellets, your bones
fractured into matchsticks.
Or they might grab you by your neck
and settle you into their aerie,
feed you bugs and berries.
Would they chain you to their fingers,
let you hover like kites in the wind?
Cage and coax you to sing?
Teach you to swear, or recite
blasphemous prayers? Or perch you
on their shoulders and show you off to their friends,
the owls or common starlings.
Imagine a murmuration of them
wiping out the sky.

BLUEBERRY CREEK

> *What would the world be, once bereft*
> *Of wet and of wildness? Let them be left*
> *O let them be left, wildness and wet*
> *Long live the weeds and the wilderness yet.*
> Gerard Manley Hopkins, "Inversnaid"

Mornings I walked, with the dog
and a small grey fog of a cat, following the creek
to where it met the river, the Columbia,
and on its banks, my small red house.
Past salal and cottonwood, the creek
spoke its noisy spring language: water
over pebble, waterfalling down ledges, and the river
answered its deep largo music.
The wide river, the noisy creek, the dog, the cat—
What would the world be, once bereft

of willow and alder, lupin
bluing the hillside, and down near the bank,
sedge grass and scrub. My boots squelching
on riparian pathways, call of an owl
on the early morning wind. The creek widens
below the house, opens to the river,
so wide the far shore dims and fades.
And what would we have done, after office and traffic,
without the owl, the grasses, the sounds
of wet and of wildness? Let them be left

though that was long ago and the house
has been razed or maybe renovated, and I live
in the city, where owls are rare and the wind
blows eerie through the telephone wires.
Creeks here are roped and tidied, their banks
not clustered with fern but walled with rock
or tucked under roads. No chance to wander

barefoot along the stream beds, balance
on boulders, hair tangled with willow branch—
O let them be left, wildness and wet

The bogs, the small creeks running,
the mountain streams crashing over rock
or trickling summerly, rainbow trout running
under lucent water, the salmon spawning
in the river, children racing the banks,
and let them know to bless the fish
in the rivers, the bear behind the trees,
the orca jumping in the Salish sea, the water
they can still cup in their hands and drink from the holy streams—
Long live the weeds and the wilderness yet.

BLESSINGS EVERY DAY

Waking up in the morning
              a blessing
Knees working
              a blessing
The first tomato, even if the only one
              a blessing

The toothbrush left behind by my grandson
              a blessing
Echo of the last notes of his improvised piano work
              a blessing
Even the emptied-out fridge
              a blessing

Books piled on counters and beds and tables
              a blessing
The television not working tonight
              a blessing
The evening phone call with my 106-year-old mother
              a hard-to-hear blessing

So many blessings, this poem could be endless
but I will end it here—
              a blessing.

FRAGILITY

1
One winter, a mushroom
shoved its way through the asphalt
in our driveway.

2
Chazak, Joshua told his troops,
so few against the enemy,
Be strong
and of good courage.

3
My mother on her daily walk,
trips on the curb,
taken to the hospital.
Nothing broken or sprained,
a little bruised, a black eye. The next day,
looking in the mirror, forgetting,
calls 911: I must have fallen.

4
Who is the biggest killer
of them all? Shark? Tiger? Man?
No, the mosquito.

5
Be the willow,
not the oak.

6
Flowers everywhere,
every vase filled.
Daffodils from the garden,
tulips from the florist.
Such a short time
of yellow.

7
These days, the big killer
is even smaller, nano-sized,
spiky, not really dead or alive.
We will beat it
by doing nothing. Staying
home, lying on the couch.

8
Shakespeare: *To love that well
which thou must leave, ere long.*

9
What is fragile: kneecaps,
fingers, love affairs,
banks, nail polish, coral reefs,
the economy.

10
Yeats: *all things fall and are built again.*
Warsaw. Coventry. Dresden. London.
Kyiv, Palmyra, Aleppo?

11
The hawthorn in the garden
hasn't put out leaves or blossoms
in years. Now beside it,
a cedar sapling from somewhere,
and another hawthorn, bursting and green.

12
How will we build again?
After we open doors,
breathe the newly washed air,
the clarified mountains,
hear the blackbird's morning song—
the once empty streets
now filled with pedestrians, and tables
under wide summer umbrellas.

RUBUS ARMENIACUS

1

The Himalayan blackberry that grows in backyards, vacant lots, lanes and alleys, that twines around the hawthorn, over rock beds, in tiny spots between buildings. An invasive species, it has taken over my backyard and the cycling paths. Cut back, it grows again like yesterday's rumour. Dug up, it finds roots to start again. Fully armoured, its thorns are spikier than roses, a gauntlet thrown in the face of city planners and horticulturalists. The worst tease, its juiciest ones hidden behind swords and daggers. Yet every morning, walking to the gym, I reach in. I love how the berries pace themselves in the bush—early green, almost ripe red, then the blackest, ready for picking. They will last me all summer, a handful at a time. I ignore the scratches to get at that one, and that one, and just one more, and this is the last.

2

One summer, anchored in Tod Inlet, we rowed to shore behind Butchart Gardens. Like abandoned children, the blackberries lingered at the edges, multiplying. We armed ourselves in denim and gloves and picked through the hot afternoon, baskets hauled across the water. Blackberry juice tainted fingers and chins and t-shirts. Blackberry pies, blackberry crisps and cobblers, blackberries on cereal, floating in milk, blackberry cordial, blackberry tarts, blackberries popped into mouths before words could emerge.

3

Blackberry, your name is exuberance, prolificate—you, and the 350,000 species of beetle. How you fill the fields, not with lilies but billions of *drupelets*, each clustered into one berry that I stuff into my mouth with my stained and blackened hands. Oh monster of excess, oh holy surfeit.

KINDERGARDENER

I am learning names, I am learning patience.
I am learning aphid and blight and spot and rot,
I am learning sun and shade and water and nutrient.
I am sprinkling, I am coaxing, I am thinning, I am cleaning.
I am praying for rain, I am praising the sun.
I am down on my knees, my hands are dirty.

VI

POMEGRANATE

for Wendy Morton

1

Seeds, carefully scooped
from their tight nest.
Nail polish red, apple of paradise red,
don't give a damn red, brothel red,
her price is above rubies red.
That red.

2

There is a trick to opening one:
first, slice off the top, under the stem,
and the fruit opens neatly
into eight sections, each covered by its white
translucent blanket. Little jewels
coaxed into a bowl, onto the yoghurt,
into the mouth. The juice,
red toothed, crunch of the seed.

3

The rabbis say there are 613 seeds,
like the 613 mitzvahs, deeds
to guide your days. Written in the Torah,
248 dos and 365 don'ts.
Do not gossip. Do not testify falsely.
Respect your parents. Do not insult anyone.
Do not engage in astrology.
Rest on the seventh day.

4

The rabbis suggest that the tree
in the middle of the Garden was not
an apple but a pomegranate. How much longer
a time from ignorance to knowledge,
from innocence to sin. Time to contemplate

this seminal action. Eve sitting down in the grass,
struggling to cut through the thick skin,
soon covered in pomegranate blood. An apple
is so much faster, a quick bite,
not a careful, tool-required, pull-out-each-seed
one-at-a-time, premeditated temptation.
And why not? the mysterious Fall,
the necessary path outward, from garden
to desert, from shelter to storm,
still red-handed.

5
I offer a pomegranate to my grandson,
age five. Here's how you open it,
I show him, and he gets to work
patiently pulling out each seed.
We are bloodied by juice
on the floor, on the counter, our hands
murdering the fruit.

6
My fingers mistype the word each time:
poemagranate. The poem inside the fruit.
Delicious words I feed to my grandson:
Raven. Hawthorn. Oregon junco.
Metaphor. Migratory. Persimmon.
words in our mouths,
            six hundred and thirteen of them.

QUAKER SERVICE, ARGENTA

A hand-built lodge on Kootenay Lake.
Sunday morning. Water lapping the shore,

a crow, singing into the silence,
wind through the maples.

March, a fire in the fireplace,
dry logs, crackling. A cough. A sigh.

The Quakers also sing into their silence:
Abide with Me. Voices join each other

in harmony. They are familiar with these words
though I am not. Not even Christian,

though the tears fall anyway. Someone
offers a Kleenex. But there is no sorrow here

only an unexpected joy—
in my language, *simcha*,

in other languages, *yorokobi, alegria,
Freude, radost*. Only words, but nothing

like the bubbly, yeasty thing that rises from nowhere
and has no provenance.

Thirteen Ways to Encounter God

I
Lay your head upon a stone,
a pillow of rock.
Dream of ladders, *sulam*, a staircase.

II
The beard, the white robes,
the hand raised in judgment,
the maleness of Him. It won't do.

III
Sunday morning on Kootenay Lake,
a Quaker meeting at Argenta.
Sun, burnished blue.
What is it that fills me with joy?

IV
It helps to have a practice.
Ride a bike, sit in lotus, write in your journal.
It helps to find a silence—
in the forest, at a park, in a quiet corner
of the library.
Who is speaking?

V
Search for her, for *Shekhinah*, who has vanished
from your world. In the jeweled and ivory palace
she lives a narrow life. Yearn for her,
take this longing with every step through the forest.
Do not lie down by the wine-red lake.
Do not reach for the apples in the tree. Eyes open
in the wilderness.

VI
Have faith, *emunah*,
in your head, in your heart, in your gut.
The thing that moves your foot each heavy step.
Some call it hope. How do you find it?
Can it be taught? I am a slow learner.

VII
Every day, a hummingbird on a branch of hawthorn.
On my birthday, two, where usually there is one.
Coincidence? Mere loveliness? A sign?
Coincidence is a spiritual pun

VIII
Every night, I recite a brief version of the *Shema*.
Then a prayer for my niece: heal her cancer.
A prayer for my family in Sweden: keep them safe.

IX
Blessing in winter:
one yellow crocus under the snow.

X
Ayecha? Where are you in the world?
At the table, with my mother,
learning patience. *Ayecha?*
tongue-tied with my daughter.
Ayecha? By the ruby lake,
fast asleep.

XI
A stone, a pillow, a place.
God was here and I did not know it.

XII
The raven flies over the hills.
Sun on the lake. A stirring in the leaves.
The wind.
Hineni. I am here.

XIII
It begins with wonder.
It begins with praise.
It begins with gratitude:
green leaves after a long winter,
daughter returning home.

SELF-PORTRAIT AROUND THE HOUSE

"Everything you do, you do in the way you do everything"
Jerry Rothstein

Garden

It was a late bloomer,
this tiny garden. Because deer.
Then a friend built a fence for her
around the patio,
and a random assortment of pots
sprouted sweet peas, roses, strawberries,
tomatoes and tulips—
the deer's favourites.
Not a garden researched and planned,
chosen because of names
(Poet's Wife, a pink tea rose),
or heritage (Black Krim tomatoes).
Learning the hard way,
squash eaten by slugs, roses by aphids,
soil needing to be turned and replenished.
Mistakes building into lessons,
but everything a wonder.
New leaves with their small soil hats
bursting out of peat pots.

Kitchen

Rainbowed ceramic knives from Costco
that can't be sharpened and don't work well,
and one bread knife, all-purpose. Le Creuset pots
in red and green, burnt at the bottoms
while she daydreams or reads.
One iron skillet that works for everything.
Cookbooks she never opens,
uses one recipe for cookies, one for cake.
One-of-a-kind dinner plates,
long stemmed champagne glasses

left over from a marriage. She never learned,
never taught her daughter
the Joy of Cooking.

Bedroom

She chose the smaller room,
enough for a bed, a dresser, a closet.
Nothing to celebrate here
but sleep and an assortment of black sweaters.
She painted the walls butterscotch,
the trim white. Hung original paintings
and framed photographs—
daughter, grandson, parents.
Beside the bed, a mountain of books,
pen and paper, a glass of water.
She has learned to stretch out in bed,
not the fetal curl of those early months
after he left.

Office

She sits on a pink exercise ball—
ergonomically correct—
in front of the computer.
Bookshelves behind and in front of her,
a window seat with books on the sill,
two large toy drawers underneath
for her grandson.
Morning and evening she types out her poems,
wonders why, these days,
she writes in third person—
is she hiding? Her personal self
locked in one of the drawers of her desk,
too embarrassed to appear? Point of view:
one more tool she can use, does she choose it?
Or is it random, like the plants in their pots,

the dishes on the shelves, the pillows
thrown onto the couch. The choices she makes—
what she keeps, what she crosses out,
the static verb she tosses for one with energy,
the excess adjectives. Will others approve?
she frets, those who might hear, might read.
Is it the truth? Leaves it in.

Nevertheless

we are saying thank you faster and faster
with nobody listening we are saying thank you
we are saying thank you and waving
dark though it is
W.S. Merwin "Thanks"

For the brief snowfall that salts the cedar branch,
for the rain that follows,
for daffodils straining to lift their green hoods,
for cut tulips on the pine table,
for the few days left until spring,
for the light lingering a bit longer each day
and Christmas lights still sparkling on the plane trees,
for brief moments of sunshine
through dark cloud, for the scent of things to come
we are saying thank you faster and faster

because nothing lasts. The hard lesson.
That summer riding the trains in Europe,
city squares a texture of brick
and cobblestone, the gleaming Duomo,
narrow streets where I wandered, hoping to remember.
Because one brief night in Amalfi, jasmine
and the sound of wind in the olive trees.
Nothing lasts, the colours fade like old fresco,
the taste of gelato slides from the tongue.
with nobody listening we are saying thank you

though we seldom hear the call of the roseate tern
or the piping plover, and never the ivory-billed woodpecker,
though the California condor whose huge wings shadow the hills,
returns, tentative. And though the western black rhino
is gone, and soon the northern white rhino,
Sumatran tiger, mountain gorilla—
long lists, categorized: vulnerable, threatened,
extinct. Yet each winter the hummingbird
returns to the hawthorn, the rhododendron to the bush, and
we are saying thank you and waving

to the deer nesting under the Garry oak, the rare
sharp-shinned hawk on the fencepost, the star magnolia
pressing her white blooms against the window,
to the many acts of kindness from neighbours and strangers,
to the new words on toddlers' tongues,
the cat curled under the bed, the dog at the door
hoping. To the lovers gone and the ones
who return for an occasional drink
for old time's sake. For the sake of the future
dark though it is.

DO NOT BE DAUNTED BY THE
ENORMITY OF THE WORLD'S GRIEF

You are not obligated to complete the work,
Neither are you free to abandon it
from the Talmud

Every tiny bit counts. Choose peace
in your own life. Forgive your own flailing self,
your wrinkled face, your wrecked knees.
Make friends with failure. Praise
the getting up, forgive the falling down.
Buy the electric bike, the solar roof, the heat pump.
Learn to say no quietly and yes exuberantly.
Praise the bent world, offer it
whatever solace you can.

INSTRUCTIONS FOR NOT GIVING UP

title after Ada Limón

You want to. The news every morning,
every evening. The dead tree
in the backyard that winter killed.
Your brother already giving up,
though your mother—bless her dwindling
teeth—will never. November feels like
doom, what now, the light also dwindling,
your friends beginning to leave. You plod on,
let go of your leaves, the bare skeleton
of you dances a slow dance around the room.
Wait a little, you tell yourself, as each twilight
arrives earlier. It will return, eight candles flaming,
that first evening with a few more minutes of light.

FEAST ON YOUR LIFE

You will love again the stranger who was yourself.
Give wine. Give bread. Give back your heart
to itself, to the stranger who has loved you
all your life, who knows you by heart.
Derek Walcott "Love After Love"

I'm a little sad, my friend says,
not to have a companion at this age,
and you leap to the defence of the single life,
full of lies you think you still believe in.
But to be fair, you are happy, or as happy
as you were when married. Stretched out
in a big bed, eating omelettes for dinner,
nobody but yourself to please. Accept
the body you live in, its creaks and crumbles.
You will love again the stranger who was yourself.

Remember a night in grad school,
you announced you were 'like a leaf on the river,
going where it leads.' Such innocence,
not knowing the shoals, the rocks,
the unexpected rapids. How to keep
your balance, or, pulled under, how
to surface. What led you here, now,
this moment that a poem surfaces:
something to celebrate:
Give wine. Give bread. Give back your heart

where you left it hanging, unused.
Here it is again, loving the daughter,
the grandson, the ancient mother,
the tomatoes in the garden, the cat
strolling across the yard, curling
onto the chair you sat on, the last morning
of sunlight. Dinner of shrimp salad,
almost acceptable, a glass of Pinot Gris
a toast to the journey the survival, sufficient
to itself, to the stranger who has loved you

when you were a child, hand on the barre,
practising arabesques and jettes,
and later, when you wore bell bottoms,
had long hair and many lovers,
and after, the years you brought Yeats
and Salinger and Blake and Shakespeare
to teenagers. When you nursed a daughter,
and held a grandson close. Who has loved you
through all your shoals and rapids,
all your life, who knows you by heart.

HOW TO LEAVE THIS GOOD EARTH

In attendance at death are two angels: Purah,
Angel of Forgetting, and Dumah, Angel of
Silence, helping the soul let go of the body.
Jewish folk tradition

I
Purah, the Angel of Forgetting,
carefully unties each knot that binds you,

the thin silk ones that can be whisked away,
like the addresses of homes you once lived in,

or the names of the flowers in your garden.
The names, perhaps, but not their scent,

not the bouquets you made of them each morning,
dropped them in a vase, brought them to your lover.

The difficult ones are thick like lines on a ship,
tied tightly to the bollards of your bones,

require hours of whispering in your ear,
let go, let go.

II
Early morning along the beach, tide coming in.
Sun rising and sunset. Rain, then wind.

Blue islands in the Salish Sea. Cedar and pine,
bare limbs of arbutus, sheen of rain on bark.

You think you might be able to do this,
might relinquish colour and scent and sound—

Brahms Symphony Number 2, adagio movement,
Chopin Etudes, the last notes of Beethoven sonatas,

But how to leave daughters and sons,
the grandchildren who will grow up without you?

If I could tell you I would let you know.
In the meantime, love all things,

listen carefully to the words of your children,
plant small gardens,
     hold tight.

ACKNOWLEDGEMENTS

With much appreciation to the editors of the following journals, who published these poems.

The glosa "Nevertheless," which won the Open Season Poetry Award, *The Malahat Review*, published in Spring Review 2018, Volume 202

"Thirteen Ways to Encounter God" in *The Fiddlehead*, 2019

"Blueberry Creek" in the anthology *Sweet Water: Poems for the Watersheds*, edited by Yvonne Blomer, Caitlin Press, 2019

"How Do You Pronounce Covid" (now titled "Mother, 104") in *The Malahat Review*, Volume 214, Spring 2021

"Lost Names" in *FreeFall*, Fall 2021, Volume 31 #2

"Girls' Basement Locker Room" was published in *EVENT*, Winter 2022/2023

"Quaker Service, Argenta" was named Honourable Mention in *FreeFall Magazine*'s Poetry Contest 2022

Many thanks to my editor, Patricia Young, who made editing such fun and who fixed this manuscript so magically.

Thanks to Russell Thorburn for his early enthusiasm for these poems and his constant encouragement.

To Ron Hatch of Ronsdale Press, who guided books to publication with humour and candour and decency, may his memory be a blessing.

To Patrick Lane, great teacher, such a fierce and tender mentor. I was lucky, and honoured, to have worked with him all those years. May his memory continue to be a blessing for all who knew him and all who read him and all who will.

To the Waywords, monthly meetings of poets who kept body and soul together: Yvonne and Pam and Grace and Wendy and David and Cynthia and Anne, thank you!

To all the poets in this rich community who offer friendship and inspiration, my deepest appreciation.

To Vici and Sarah and Malaika of Caitlin Press who gave these poems such a wonderful home.

To Phyllis Serota for the loan of her painting for the cover.

And to my family across the water, thank you for your love and support and for giving me such good material to write about.

Notes

Now Is the Time to Light It
Lines from this cento are borrowed from the following poems by Patrick Lane: "Moths," "God Walks Burning Through Me," "Warbler," "Kingfisher," "Lost and Found," "Palms," and "No Longer Two People." With thanks to the publishers at Harbour Publishing.

z'l is the shortened form for "may their memory be a blessing" in Hebrew.

Cello
The borrowed four lines is a poem in itself, "In A Field, at Sunset" by Carl Phillips, in Plume Issue #101, January 2020

Peaceful Easy Feeling
From The Eagles' first album, *Eagles*, 1972

Blueberries
Borrowed lines are from Laura Apol's poem "Blueberries" in *Crossing the Ladder of Sun* (Michigan State University Press, 2004).

Abject
Borrowed lines are from Jan Zwicky's the introductory poem to *Forge* (Gaspereau Press, 2011).

Beth Israel Synagogue, 1955
Hashkiveinu is a blessing of peace and was one of my father's solo parts when he was choir leader.

While Walking with My Father, Late February 2006
The coyote, from various Native American and Indigenous mythology, in particular the Maidu, is a primal being from the beginning of time, who works with Earth Maker to create the world, by singing it to life. In most stories, he is both a trickster and a benefactor to humans.

Christmas
Nes Gadol Hayah Sham is written on each side of the *dreidel,* the spinning top which is part of the Hanukah game. Translated: "a great miracle happened there," commemorating the cleansing of the Temple led by the Maccabees (approximately 160 BCE) and the miracle of the oil that lasted eight days.

Difficult Advice
Borrowed lines from various statements found in the books of Isaiah, prophet from the 8th century BCE, mainly Verses 45:7.

Aron Hakodesh, the Holy Light or Eternal Light, remains lit in every synagogue in front of the Ark which holds the Torah scrolls.

Truth
After the poem "Lies I Tell" by Sarah Borjas, originally published in Poem-a-Day on September 26, 2018, by the Academy of American Poets.

About Memory
Each of the titles of the stanzas comes from lectures by Rabbi Harry Brechner during sessions of the Calling All Artists Project, 2019, "Memory and Essence."

Star Magnolia, First Buds at my Window
Quoted line (in italics) from "Under One Small Star" by Wyslawa Szymborska.

Blueberry Creek
Borrowed lines from Gerard Manley Hopkins, "Inversnaid," 1881.

Fragility
Chazak: Hebrew for "strength." "Be strong and of good courage," Joshua to his troops, Book of Deuteronomy 23:31.

"To love that well which thou must leave ere long," William Shakespeare, Sonnet 73.

"All things fall and are built again," WB Yeats, "Lapis Lazuli."

Pomegranate
According to Jewish tradition, the Torah contains 613 commandments, or *mitzvot*. This tradition is first recorded in the 3rd century CE, when Rabbi Simlai mentioned it in a sermon that is recorded in Talmud Makkot 23b. Also in the Talmud, the rabbis suggest the fruit of The Tree in the Garden of Eden might be a pomegranate, a fruit indigenous to the area in the Middle East, which is thought to contain 613 seeds.

Thirteen Ways to Encounter God
Stanza I refers to Jacob's dream of the ladder (*sulam*) to Heaven.

Stanza III refers to Argenta, a Quaker community on the northern shore of Kootenay Lake.

Stanza VII, quotation from G.K. Chesterton, British novelist.

Stanzas V, X, XI: the story of the Lost Princess, told by Rabbi Nachum of Breslov (19th Century Hasidic rabbi). In this story, the Princess, who represents *Shekhina,* the feminine aspect of God, has disappeared into a place of "Not Good", and the King's viceroy searches for her. Endlessly. He is given many tests, all of which he fails, until finally after many, many years, finds her in an ivory palace. The Hebrew word *Ayecha,* which means "where are you in the world," refers to his confusion and his search. The word is a kind of wake-up call. The other Hebrew word, *Hineni,* which means "I am here," is used only a few times in the Bible, "here" meaning totally and completely attentive and present (the choir sings the word in Leonard Cohen's song, "You Want it Darker").

Nevertheless
Borrowed lines from W.S. Merwin "Thanks," from *Migration: New and Selected Poems*, 2005.

Do Not Be Daunted by the Enormity of the World's Grief
Quote from *Pirket Avot,* Sayings of the Fathers, loosely translated around quote from Micha 6:8

Instructions for Not Giving Up
Title borrowed from Ada Limón's poem of the same name, in *The Carrying*, 2018

Feast on Your Life
Borrowed lines from Derek Walcott, "Love After Love," included in his *Collected Poems, 1948–1984*, Farrar, Straus and Giroux, 1987.

How to Leave This Good Earth
Borrowed line from W.H. Auden's "If I Could Tell You," a villanelle written in 1940 and found in his Collected Poems, 1976.

ABOUT THE AUTHOR

JACKIE SAUNDERS-RITCHIE PHOTO

Barbara Pelman has an MA in Literature from the University of Toronto, and lives in Victoria, BC. She taught high school and university English courses for three decades and is now retired. She has three books of poetry: *One Stone* (Ekstasis Editions, 2005), *Borrowed Rooms* (Ronsdale Press, 2008) and *Narrow Bridge* (Ronsdale Press, 2017), and a chapbook, *Aubade Amalfi* (Rubicon Press, 2016). She is an active member of Victoria's vibrant poetry community, and is a frequent traveller to Vancouver to visit her family.